Prayer-treating Backward Dreams

Anthony O. Akerele

Copyright © 2012 Anthony O. Akerele

All rights reserved.

ISBN: 978-0-9837760-8-6

DEDICATION

To dreamers all over the world

CONTENTS

	Acknowledgments	i
1	Backward Dreams	8

ACKNOWLEDGMENTS

I deeply appreciate the efforts of my wife, Nnenna, to bring this book to publication. Many thanks Sweetheart.

1 BACKWARD DREAMS

Backward dreams : Anti-progress dreams

One of the most common problem I have encountered on the deliverance ground is people having backward dreams. If there are dreams that typify people who cannot make desired progress in life, backward dreams would be the most common. If there are dreams that characterize people who find themselves stagnant in the race of life, backward dreams would qualify. If there are dreams that make people scratch their heads looking for a meaning and interpretation and still find none, backward dreams would qualify. Whenever you find frustration and un-necessary struggle in a life, look closely and you will find backward dreams. These dreams must have a deep significance as we have come to know on deliverance ground. What are backward dreams?

Backward dreams are dreams in which you find yourself in the past where you started out from. You find yourself in your childhood days when you were in elementary and high schools. You would see yourself doing what you no longer do in real life. You see yourself going to those specific geographic locations you have moved away from in time and space. In backward dreams you find yourself where you have left and left for good. The frequency and the consistency of these dreams is the measure of the intensity of the message. There are those who have these dreams whenever they pray intensively and some when they hit a particular age and some when they are at the edge of breakthroughs and still some only at some seasons of the year or particular time of the year. There could be interpretations based on context in individual dreams but the core message is always the same. A summoning power at work whenever you want to breakthrough, whenever you want to break a limit placed on your bloodline, whenever you pray hard and want to make progress in life, whenever you are about to do what no one else in your father's house has ever done, whenever your salvation is being contested by the gods you longer serve because you have come to Christ, whenever those familiar with you want you stagnated so that they may get ahead of you, whenever you become the weakest link in the chain of those that must suffer an impending attack.

But let it be said why the Bible attaches great importance to dreams. All through scriptures dreams are mentioned and used by God to communicate with man. And they are often weird-sounding and weird-looking because translating spiritual elements into comprehensible physical reality will always be a hard task given the difference in the nature of both.

Numbers 12:6
And he said, Hear now my words: If there be a prophet among you, I the Lord will make myself known unto him in a vision, and will speak unto him in a dream.

Job 33:13-18
Job 33:14 For God speaketh once, yea twice, yet man perceiveth it not.

Job 33:15 In a dream, in a vision of the night, when deep sleep falleth upon men, in slumberings upon the bed;
Job 33:16 Then he openeth the ears of men, and sealeth their instruction,
Job 33:17 That he may withdraw man from his purpose, and hide pride from man.

Acts 2:17
And it shall come to pass in the last days, saith God, I will pour out of my Spirit upon all flesh: and your sons and your daughters shall prophesy, and your young men shall see visions, and your old men shall dream dreams:

The three above-referenced scriptures show the relevance of dreams to every student of advanced spiritual warfare.
Dreams are important. Abraham, Jacob, Joseph, Solomon, many Kings in the Bible like Pharaoh and Nebuchadnezzar all had dreams.
Having established the relevance of dreams in kingdom dispensation, what is the meaning of backward dreams and why many at one point or the other in their lives find themselves having these dreams? We go places because we have a need to go. We also go to places because we are summoned. We can also go to places inadvertently. The problem now arises when we repeatedly and consistently do so in the dream. This biblical interpretation of backward dreams is a protected knowledge. It may not make sense to those it has been protected from!

Summoning Powers and Basis of Summons
"Ordinarily, a summon is an order to appear before Judge or Magistrate. A summon is a command to appear. An authoritative and urgent call to someone to be present or do something. The court-issued summon

could be a writ, a subpoena, warrant, court order or citation."
To summon is to call for, to invite, to ask for, to cite authoritatively.
Many have backward dreams as a result of evil summons and this is why it is important to know how evil summons originate. Who is summoning and why? When and why is the summon a contest of your salvation? Why is the summon resulting in a backward dream?

Sources of evil summons

1. Thrones
2. Covenanted assignments coded into the blood
3. Covenant-coded blood
4. Needs, programmed and regular, can also be used to summon a person.

Thrones as sponsors of backward dreams

Ecclesiastes 8:4 (GNT) The king acts with authority, and no one can challenge what he does.

When power corrupts, power corrupts. When absolute power corrupts, absolute power corrupts absolutely. Man is fallible. When man occupies the throne, the throne is regarded infallible because the throne is owned always by deity. The Pope for example is said to be infallible when he speaks ex- cathedra, when he speaks from the throne. Every spot on earth is linked to a to a throne as every soul is also linked to throne. The power, pronouncements and decrees from local thrones, the activities of local thrones can draw you back to the domain of the throne if you are away from that domain "inappropriately". And this may result in backward dreams. This is a peek into one of most the important reason why people have backward dreams and the power acting on people to provoke such dreams.

Every soul has a connection or link to a throne just as every spot on this planet and every piece of land. The link could be direct as royalty or priesthood and indirect as just a subject of the kingdom. Democracies are nothing but thrones re-configured. Just as no piece of land is outside of jurisdiction, no soul is un-attached. Everyone has a relationship with one throne or the other. This knowledge is very vital in understanding backward dreams. There are throne exchanges and throne take-over like when a smaller throne is swallowed by a bigger throne. This happens all the time and we call it war!

The danger of course arises when the throne is abused by man, as man has often done with almost everything. How else would you explain the "kings set themselves against the Lord and against His anointed, saying let us break their bands asunder and cast away their cords from us .....". This is definitely a rebellion of kings against the Lord and against His anointed. A king that rebels against the Lord is definitely fallible. The power of the throne can be abused to have undue control and manipulation of the subjects of the throne.

The scripture that hold the secret to many backward dreams is Proverbs 14:28

Prov.14:28
Proverbs 14:28 (GNT) A king's greatness depends on how many people he rules; without them he is nothing.

What you are about to read is a protected knowledge. It may not sound knowledgeable or reasonable to you because the knowledge is protected from you. Every spot on this planet is attached to a throne either directly or indirectly. Not a single spot is outside of jurisdiction. The throne is an altar of a deity. Men do not make thrones. The gods do. If you do not believe in the existence of gods and their place in the scheme of things you will not be able to grasp the knowledge why people have backward dreams. Psalm 2 says "why do the heathen rage and the people imagine a vain thing , the kings of the earth set themselves together, against the Lord and against his anointed......" The kings of the earth that sets themselves together against the Lord and His anointed are in rebellion, hence in witchcraft. You will find Kings and Princes of certain lands like Persia and Greece mentioned in the scriptures, and the mentioned princes are certainly not flesh and blood. What earthly kings set themselves against the Lord if not the powers that have rebelled in heaven and now rule the earth through man chosen to represent their interests.

When kings rule they need subjects to do so. A king with no subject is not a king. Everything in the kingdom of a king is geared towards preserving the throne and getting more people to "cover" the throne. The cover is a defense for the throne. The culture, traditions and religion established by the throne serve innately the purpose of perpetuating the throne. There are concentric circles around the thrones made up of the royal class, the priestly class and the commons. Of course, there may be many subdivisions in each concentric circle. The closer you are to the throne the less likely you can get away from the domain of the throne without consequence. The most serious of the consequences is arrested progress or stagnancy and that is the chief feature of backward dreams. What binds the members of the royal family to the throne is stronger than what binds the members of the priesthood or the common subjects. Many today are of royal blood and they know it not. Many are of the priestly blood. The commons are like slaves and servants to the throne and this is also a reason why they cannot just abandon the throne without consequence.

The corruption and abuse associated with the throne has been aptly described in the scriptures.

1Samuel 8

5 And said unto him, Behold, thou art old, and thy sons walk not in thy ways: now make us a king to judge us like all the nations.
6 But the thing displeased Samuel, when they said, Give us a king to judge us. And Samuel prayed unto the Lord.
7 And the Lord said unto Samuel, Hearken unto the voice of the people in all that they say unto thee: for they have not rejected thee, but they have rejected me, that I should not reign over them.
8 According to all the works which they have done since the day that I brought them up out of Egypt even unto this day, wherewith they have forsaken me, and served other gods, so do they also unto thee.
9 Now therefore hearken unto their voice: howbeit yet protest solemnly unto them, and shew them the manner of the king that shall reign over them.
10 And Samuel told all the words of the Lord unto the people that asked of him a king.
11 And he said, This will be the manner of the king that shall reign over you: He will take your sons, and appoint them for himself, for his chariots, and to be his horsemen; and some shall run before his chariots.
12 And he will appoint him captains over thousands, and captains over fifties; and will set them to ear his ground, and to reap his harvest, and to make his instruments of war, and instruments of his chariots.
13 And he will take your daughters to be confectionaries, and to be cooks, and to be bakers.
14 And he will take your fields, and your vineyards, and your oliveyards, even the best of them, and give them to his servants.
15 And he will take the tenth of your seed, and of your vineyards, and give to his officers, and to his servants.

16 And he will take your menservants, and your maidservants, and your goodliest young men, and your asses, and put them to his work.
17 He will take the tenth of your sheep: and ye shall be his servants.
18 And ye shall cry out in that day because of your king which ye shall have chosen you; and the Lord will not hear you in that day.
19 Nevertheless the people refused to obey the voice of Samuel; and they said, Nay; but we will have a king over us;

The king, according to this scripture, will take the sons and daughters of his subjects for his own personal profit. Everything the throne does is to preserve the throne. Much of the activities of the throne are done out of the need to protect and preserve the throne. Every spot on earth is subjected to a throne. And do not be deceived our so called democracies are nothing but the "throne re-configured". The gods through a man taking service and therefore worship from another man.
The throne exercises this power through covenant and dedication rituals that involves blood. Just as Moses in Exodus 24 uses the blood from blood sacrifice to bind and dedicate the people of Israel to God so also the thrones use blood sacrifice to tie, bind and dedicate people to the throne. This is to keep souls attached to the throne. This is often culturally and traditionally done by way of local feasts and festivals. Every throne, therefore every deity has feasts and festivals just like the feasts associated with the Tabernacle of the Living God.
The blood covenants and dedications rituals mark the blood of the subjects of the throne to keep them from leaving the domain of the throne such that if they do leave, there will be backward dreams to stop them, to stagnate them and arrest their progress. This is not all. If the subjects leave the religion associated with the throne, the new religion of the subject will be highly

contested all in the bid not to lose subjects. Battles of contested salvation in the life of new converts can be likened to the struggles experienced by Israel in exodus from Egypt under the guidance of the Almighty God but still pursued by Pharaoh, still showing nostalgia for lifestyle of Egypt.

Matthew Henry's commentary on Proverbs 14:28 is an eye-opener:

"Here are two maxims in politics, which carry their own evidence with them: - 1. That it is much for the honour of a king to have a populous kingdom; it is a sign that he rules well, since strangers are hereby invited to come and settle under his protection and his own subjects live comfortably; it is a sign that he and his kingdom are under the blessing of God, the effect of which is being fruitful and multiplying. It is his strength, and makes him considerable and formidable; happy is the king, the father of his country, who has his quiver full of arrows; he shall not be ashamed, but shall speak with his enemy in the gate, Psa 127:4, Psa 127:5. It is therefore the wisdom of princes, by a mild and gentle government, by encouraging trade and husbandry, and by making all easy under them, to promote the increase of their people. And let all that wish well to the kingdom of Christ, and to his honour, do what they can in their places that many may be added to his church. 2. That when the people are lessened the prince is weakened: In the want of people is the leanness of the prince (so some read it); trade lies dead, the ground lies untilled, the army wants to be recruited, the navy to be manned, and all because there are not hands sufficient. See how much the honour and safety of kings depend upon their people, which is a reason why they should rule by love, and not with rigour. Princes are corrected by those judgments which abate the number of the people, as we find, 2Sa 24:13."

The earthly throne, like everything Satan does, is sustained and powered by witchcraft, ..."the kings set themselves together against the Lord and against His anointed......". Throne magic and throne witchcraft must be addressed to put and end to backward dreams, especially when they recur from battles of contested salvation. The throne has worked witchcraft to make sure it does not lose subjects or officials by covenanting and dedicating many offices, duties and loyalties. Your blood is a marked record. The blood does not lie! And it cannot lie. The life is in the blood. Addressing the power of the throne to summon with warfare prayers will provoke dramatic breakthroughs as backward dreams are prayer-treated.

Take these prayers :
Throne magic, throne witchcraft summoning me backwards, release me and die, I have come to Christ.

Throne magic, throne witchcraft I break your chains in the name of Jesus.

Covenanted-assignments as sponsors of backward dreams

A Sister brought her fiancee to a pre-wedding counseling session. The man is a lawyer. He moved to United States from Europe, he was born and grew up in Nigeria. At a precise time in the US, the backward dreams started and repeated itself for a while to come. He would consistently find himself in his place of origin and would be looking for documents to travel out of his place of origin to where he is today, and was never able to get the documents that was required to travel out and of course always to his frustration, he could never get to leave his place of origin in the dreams. Though he is in the US but in the dream he would plan to go to the US but could never make it. Guess what? In real life his situation in his present location begs for explanation given his education and expectations. He was not making progress at all. Anti-progress powers have shown up in the backward dreams. Upon a few questions it came to be that his blood, his family were the custodian of the oracles of his place of origin. This simply means that his family, his bloodline must furnish priesthood to the local throne and the corresponding deity. And because of this, his blood is covenanted and dedicated to the local priesthood that caters to the local throne. The knowledge to break away from the anti-progress powers was protected from him. His level of education made him to disbelieve the things of the spirit. The more educated we become the more difficult to believe the things of the spirit. He could not tie the backward dreams to his priesthood lineage. As a matter of fact he has a disdain for the priesthood as practiced by his father's house. The dreams started when he hit the age of becoming a priest of the gods of the land. The Levites get to serve when they hit 30-years old. The age Jesus began his ministry.

- "Take a head count of the Kohathites, who are part of the Levites, by their clans and patriarchal houses, of those 30 years of age until 50 years of age, all who are eligible for performing assigned tasks in the work force pertaining to the Tent of Meeting" (Num 4:3)
- "Take a head count of the Gershonite clans as well, by their clans and patriarchal houses. You shall tally all of them 30 years of age and older to 50 years of age, all who are eligible to perform the tasks of the work force relevant to the Tent of Meeting" (Num 4:23)
- "Take a head count of the Merarites, 30 years of age and older…" (Num 4:30)

In Kingdom economy, there is time for everything and there is division of labor. In Kingdom space there is appointed place and there is neither fulfillment nor prosperity outside of your appointed place. Our God is a

God of order. The twelve tribes of Israel have their appointed space around the central Tabernacle and in the promised land they have their designated cities, where they are free to exercise rights of ownership. A member of the tribe of Judah cannot go exercise rights in the place allocated to the tribe of Gad! Prosperity and fulfillment will fail you if you are outside of your divinely allocated and appointed place. Many struggle unnecessarily because they are outside of their appointed place.

The brother started having backward dreams when he hit a particular age, which of course coincided with the age of ordination and initiation into the local priesthood of his place of origin. When you have backward dreams, every of your incoming breakthrough will be threatened with abortion! Helpers will be hard to find when you have backward dreams.
Many will have backward dreams when they hit the age to serve in certain roles or offices that are regulated by blood covenant or dedication to the throne of their place of origin. The dream may continue for a period that may tally for the period of ordination or consecration and that, in many cases, may go from a few weeks to years. Concentric circles of the royal family, families of the priesthood and the common subjects surround every throne. The throne is a highly spiritual manifestation representing a deity. And I mean every throne. Throne is never made by man but by the gods and so the activities of the throne are highly spiritual. The assignments given out by the throne for the preservation of the throne are also spiritual. This is why the activities of the thrones are highly ritualized.

Backward dreams sponsored by covenanted assignments are the evidences that the place you have left requires your presence to fulfill throne-assigned or deity-assigned roles, offices or duties. Many people have been summoned back when the local deity has placed a call or summon on them.

Another sister ran into so much turbulence in her marriage, a recently contracted marriage, because of a suddenly developed uncontrollable temper that she could no longer manage. Not long after, she received a message that she has been chosen as the wife of the local deity of her place of origin and as long as she is not responding to the call, the temper would be always uncontrollable. Covenants and dedications coded into the blood have power to enforce judgment. Backward dreams would feature prominently in her dream life running up to this event in her marriage. Backward dreams is a sign of brewing and ongoing battles in the spirit. It should be taken seriously.

Assignments that summon......It was her family turn to provide a wife to the idol of their town. And she was chosen by divination, though she was hundreds of miles away in another city entirely. The time has come for her to become wife of the deity.
There are assignments you receive by virtue of your name and blood. At the appointed time, backward dreams may begin. Some were slated to die with the King. Their name portrays their fatal duty. Everyone with the name have the blood coded with the covenant.

Covenant-coded Blood that summons
The blood can be covenant-coded, meaning a covenant can be spiritually written into your blood. A covenant cut or made with blood can always be translated into a covenant that can be written or coded into your blood because of the principle of like begets like, deep calleth deep. Since the establishment of the ruling class and the priesthood, both of which constitute the elite of every society, the largest class, which is the class of the common people, is spiritually demarcated by covenants coded into the blood. This is the reason why no blood of just any Israelite would meet the requirements laid by the Gibeonites except the blood of Saul. The blood of who killed the Gibeonites.

2 Samuel 21:1-6

Then there was a famine in the days of David three years, year after year; and David enquired of the Lord. And the Lord answered, It is for Saul, and for his bloody house, because he slew the Gibeonites.

² And the king called the Gibeonites, and said unto them; (now the Gibeonites were not of the children of Israel, but of the remnant of the Amorites; and the children of Israel had sworn unto them: and Saul sought to slay them in his zeal to the children of Israel and Judah.)

³ Wherefore David said unto the Gibeonites, What shall I do for you? and wherewith shall I make the atonement, that ye may bless the inheritance of the Lord?

⁴ And the Gibeonites said unto him, We will have no silver nor gold of Saul, nor of his house; neither for us shalt thou kill any man in Israel. And he said, What ye shall say, that will I do for you.

⁵ And they answered the king, The man that consumed us, and that devised against us that we should be destroyed from remaining in any of the coasts of Israel,

⁶ Let seven men of his sons be delivered unto us, and we will hang them up unto the Lord in Gibeah of Saul,

whom the Lord did choose. And the king said, I will give them.

It was covenant-coded blood of Saul, that singled out those that must be killed to appease the Gibeonites and restore rain to end the famine in Israel. The grandson of Saul were not spared. Your blood can be used to single you out.

Where my blood has been used to single me out for tragedy and disaster, blood of Jesus stand for me, in the name of Jesus.

Blood of Jesus, remove and replace my blood whenever my blood is about to respond to evil summons, in the name of Jesus.

Powers using my blood to summon me backward, my blood has become the blood of Jesus and cannot be summoned, in the name of Jesus.

Dark covenants in my blood identifying me for darkness, break by the blood of Jesus in the name of Jesus.

By this same token, blood can be used to locate those that can be summoned backward. If you are having backward dreams, your blood may carry what is allowing you to be located for this summon backward. Backward dreams are consequences of evil summons.

The same reason why some people are categorized and classified outcast by covenants the whole society agrees to. In the Indian society, the caste system is regulated by covenants coded into the blood unbeknownst to most people. How does your blood get codified with covenants? Codification of covenants into the blood is visible from Exodus 24. Moses was basically using blood sacrifice to codify covenants into the blood of the children of Israel.

Exodus 24:6-8

⁶ And Moses took half of the blood, and put it in basons; and half of the blood he sprinkled on the altar.

⁷ And he took the book of the covenant, and read in the audience of the people: and they said, All that the Lord hath said will we do, and be obedient.

⁸ And Moses took the blood, and sprinkled it on the people, and said, Behold the blood of the covenant, which the Lord hath made with you concerning all these words.

Every Israelite present at this transaction and their unborn children would have their blood spoken to in this blood sprinkling transaction. The covenant they just agreed to will be spoken into their blood by the sprinkling of the blood by Moses. The Lord will hereafter always refer to this covenant codification procedure to hold Israel responsible. The book of Hebrews 8:8-9 commented:

Hebrews 8:8-9

⁸ For finding fault with them, he saith, Behold, the days come, saith the Lord, when I will make a new covenant with the house of Israel and with the house of Judah:

⁹ Not according to the covenant that I made with their fathers in the day when I took them by the hand to lead

them out of the land of Egypt; because they continued not in my covenant, and I regarded them not, saith the Lord.

The fathers and generations yet unborn have their blood covenant-codified and the blood would always be used to hold them responsible. Whenever you are having backward dreams, you are simply being called through your blood to either royal or priesthood assignments and possibly communal assignments. When Americans get to a particular age, they can be called into military service and not before that age. That duty can be used to summon also in the spirit in such a way that it would make those not responding to start having backward dreams. These dreams are to let you know that your attention is spiritually required somewhere else than where you are. The enemy plays into this to carry out his agenda to steal, kill and destroy.

The core message of backward dreams
Your identity is carried in your blood. Everybody's blood is marked by covenant and dedication rituals. The blood of every soul on earth, by covenant would belong to one of these three classes of 1. the throne, 2. the priesthood and 3. the commons. Every class or category with its own duties and responsibilities. Most of these duties and responsibilities are age-related and the covenants or agreements that established them are done often on the basis of age. If your next birthday is the age at which people with your blood enter into the priesthood, backward dreams may begin to appear. Souls may mingle and mix all they want, they are presorted by the covenants and dedication rituals attaching them to thrones. Even democracies are re-configured thrones. The law of the last boundary, the last altar, the last throne is valid in the sorting of souls. Souls are always being handed over from one throne to higher throne all the time. When so many Syrians migrated to Germany

because of civil war in Syria, thrones were in souls-handing-over transactions spiritually. The throne of Syria was handing souls over to the throne of Germany in the spirit realm. The Syrians that would rather be in Germany rather than Turkey or Greece were enrolling themselves by their preference for Germany. They agreed within themselves to go to Germany. Thrones traded them spiritually unbeknownst to them. Thrones control souls. Thrones must not be left empty. This principle is now fed into the agenda of the prince of this world to steal, kill and destroy. Souls can by this set up be stagnated to arrest progress and steal, kill and destroy. Backward dreams will slow you down to a screeching halt in the race of life.

There is a summoning ritual of roasted yam employed by some ethnic groups. It involves roasting a yam tuber and attaching the name of the summoned to the roasted yam. While the yam is on fire, the name of who is to be summoned is invoked by calling the name to come for the roasted yam. " John the son of Doe, this is your roasted yam, do not tarry, appear and eat your yam." It is believed by this ethnic group, that the yam once in the fire with a name attached, the one summoned cannot reject the call to eat roasted yam. The summoned will suddenly develop a great urge to show up at the point of invocation, irrespective of distance. Such a ritual can be worked out of wickedness to provoke backward dreams.

Need
A need in your life, the need for a breakthrough, fruitfulness, healing, deliverance can be used to draw someone to a river or sea or shrine for a ritual. This is a form of evil summon when you find yourself in the dream going repeatedly to a place because of a need in

your life. A tire repair shop throwing nails on the road to puncture people's car tires right before they get to the shop, is programming a need that will bring people to his shop. The idols and gods can make you barren to make you seek their help to overcome barrenness through your worship of the idols and gods. This may be initiated in your dreams as backward dreams insofar they act from your place of origin that you may have left or moved away from.

Effects of Backward Dreams
The effects of backward dreams can be devastating. A brother was in need of a document of breakthrough that eluded him for over 30 years. And that is how long he has been having these dreams. After 30 years, when he finally got a seeming breakthrough to get the documents, an inexplicable disappointment at the very last minute threw him back to square one. He testified of the breakthrough only to have his testimony reversed. Only now that he has come to deliverance ground to gain this knowledge of backward dreams and began to prayer-treat the backward dreams is he finally getting a divine assurance that basically comes from the likes of the prayers in this book and true faith in God.

The effects of backward dreams include:
Stagnancy
Slow progress
Frustration
Failure in what you know how to do
Disappointment especially in relationships
The past always catching up with you
Disfavor
Lack of helpers where it matters most
Rejection to make you go backward

If you find these above-mentioned situations in your life and you are having backward dreams, then know for sure that the dreams are satanically powered. And the prayers below or rather the answers to the prayers below will convince you.

How to stop backward dreams

Only God the Father, God the Son and God the Holy Spirit can stop backward dreams. Especially when the enemy is bent on getting your attention with it. And this cannot be done except you have a relationship with Christ. The prince of this world would always have sway over his subjects until Christ takes you out of the domain of the enemy by calling you out of the world. Accept the call of Christ right now by accepting Christ as your Lord and Savior through confession of your sins and repenting and renouncing the sins of your life in the name of Jesus. Then and only then can you begin the warfare prayers below to kill backward dreams.

The knowledge background of a decree is very important if you are to derive the full benefit of the decree. These decrees derive from the knowledge expounded above. It is vital to gain knowledge if you aspire to deliverance. The acquisition of knowledge is always sacrificial and sacrifice is always a generator of power. Either good or evil.

Prayers below are best taken between 12midnight and 3am.

PRAYERS
1. Let the invocation of my name to summon me backward, die in the name of Jesus.
2. Who is invoking my name to summon me backward, let your power die in the name of Jesus.

3. Throne magic, throne witchcraft sponsoring backward dreams in my life, die in the name of Jesus
4. Throne magic, throne witchcraft, throne wickedness affecting my life, die in the name of Jesus.
5. Throne magic, throne witchcraft, throne wickedness, I break your chains in the name of Jesus.
6. Invisible bondages tying me down to the past, I break your chains in the name of Jesus.
7. I reject anti-kingdom assignments employed to call me backward in my dreams, in the name of Jesus.
8. Satanic assignment that awaits those that turn the age of my next birthday in my father's house, I reject you in the name of Jesus.
9. Anti-progress powers in my dream, die with your accomplishments in my dream in the name of Jesus.
10. Powers summoning me backwards to arrest my progress, die in the name of Jesus.
11. Summoning rituals carried out by those familiar with me to punish me, backfire in the name of Jesus.
12. Consequence of anti-progress dreams be reversed in the name of Jesus.
13. Consequence of evil dreams, be reversed
14. Satanic assignments employed to summon me backward, lose your hold upon my life in the name of Jesus.
15. Evil sacrifice offered to arrest my progress in life, be overruled by the sacrifice of Christ.
16. Power of evil sacrifice behind my case, die!!!
17. Evil blood sacrifice offered to keep stubborn situation in place in my life, die in the name of Jesus.
18. Evil summon calling me away when good things are about to happen, backfire!!

19. Power of evil summon at the edge of my breakthrough, die in the name of Jesus
20. Satanic assignments given to me by virtue of my name, I refuse and I reject in the name of Jesus.
21. Satanic assignments given to me by virtue of my blood, I refuse and I reject in the name of Jesus.
22. Every desire given to me to work shame and disgrace in my life, let the desire die, in the name of Jesus.
23. Power of great mistakes programmed to work shame and disgrace in my life, let the power die in the name of Jesus.
24. Camp of those waiting for my mistake, wait in vain and wait disappointed in the name of Jesus.
25. Blood of Jesus cut off now the flow of wickedness available to my enemies, in the name of Jesus.
26. Who is putting a garment of shame on me, wear your garment in the name of Jesus.
27. The garment of shame put on me in the dream, Holy Ghost tear it off in the name of Jesus.
28. Who is praying on my pictures to put me to shame, let your power die, in the name of Jesus.
29. Every battle of "I told you so", programmed to put me to shame, backfire! In the name of Jesus.
30. Battles of what shall I do, come to an end in my life, marriage and career in the name of Jesus.
31. I reject every satanic assignments given by evil thrones in the name of Jesus.
32. I reject every race without a prize
33. Assignments by appointments from evil thrones, scatter in the name of Jesus.
34. I acknowledge and I thank you Lord for the grace that has given me all I have and made me all I am.
35. Holy Spirit! capture every evil assignments before I accept it.

36. Every satanic law sustaining evil assignments in my life, break down in the name of Jesus.
37. Every assignment given to me not by God to disgrace me, let the assignment die in the name of Jesus.
38. Every satanic assignment to stagnate my destiny, backfire in the name of Jesus.
39. Every assignment programmed to bite me like a serpent, bite your owner in the name of Jesus.
40. Every assignment that will take me into the enemy's camp, I reject it, Holy Ghost revoke it, in the name of Jesus.
41. Who is using my blood to give me a satanic assignment, let your power die in the name of Jesus.
42. The assignment given to me by the spirit spouse and some other deities of my fathers house that will not allow me to leave and cleave die and backfire in the name of Jesus.
43. Every assignment given to me by the gods and idols of my father's house to rubbish my destiny backfire and die in the name of Jesus.
44. Powers putting evil load into my hands to make me spiritually busy so that I cannot fulfill my destiny take your load and die in the name of Jesus.
45. Idols I have set up, idols set up on my behalf, let your altars die in the name of Jesus.
46. Where my blood has been used to single me out for tragedy and disaster, blood of Jesus stand for me, in the name of Jesus.
47. Blood of Jesus, remove and replace my blood whenever my blood is about to respond to evil summons, in the name of Jesus.
48. Powers using my blood to summon me backward, my blood has become the blood of Jesus and cannot be summoned, in the name of Jesus.

49. Dark covenants in my blood identifying me for darkness, break by the blood of Jesus in the name of Jesus.
50. Powers that have come for payment for what I did not buy and have taken my progress, die and release my progress in the name of Jesus.

References
Henry Matthew's Commentary

ABOUT THE AUTHOR

Anthony Akerele is a Geologist by profession and a ministering "Priest and King" at the Mountain of Fire and Miracles Ministries Virginia, in Springfield, Virginia. He is the author of "Command the Month @ The Midnight Gate". He is happily married to Nnenna with children. They are both permanently enrolled in the Holy Spirit's end-time Army.

www.ingramcontent.com/pod-product-compliance
Lightning Source LLC
Chambersburg PA
CBHW061315040426
42444CB00010B/2645